FOREWORD

The tie as we know it today has its origins in the second half of the 17th century in France, thanks to Croatian mercenaries, they in their traditional costumes used a white cloth called HRVATSKA, which was knotted in the shape of a rose and its Limbs dangled on their breasts. The French liked this HRVATSKA very much and they started using it daily calling it cravate.

Later at the end of the same century the French began to gently tie this tie around their necks using clasps.

During the French Revolution, the tie became a symbol of status and political power, where the revolutionary wore black ties while the counterrevolutionaries wore white.

In Napoleon's time he always wore a black tie with white edges, until on the morning of June 18, 1815 he decided to change his tie, losing that day the Battle of Waterloo. From this moment on, the art of knotting a piece of cloth around the neck has become an elegant sign of men's clothing.

Currently the tie is used to give a touch of formality in different areas, For example, in the courts of law its use is practically mandatory, however, companies led by young people do not use this accessory.

SIMPLE KNOT

This knot is also known as a four-turn knot and consists of a simple, narrow and asymmetrical knot, ideal for standard button-down shirts, and is recommended for wide ties, suitable for casual events

- Esthetic - ☆☆☆☆
- Difficulty - ☆☆☆

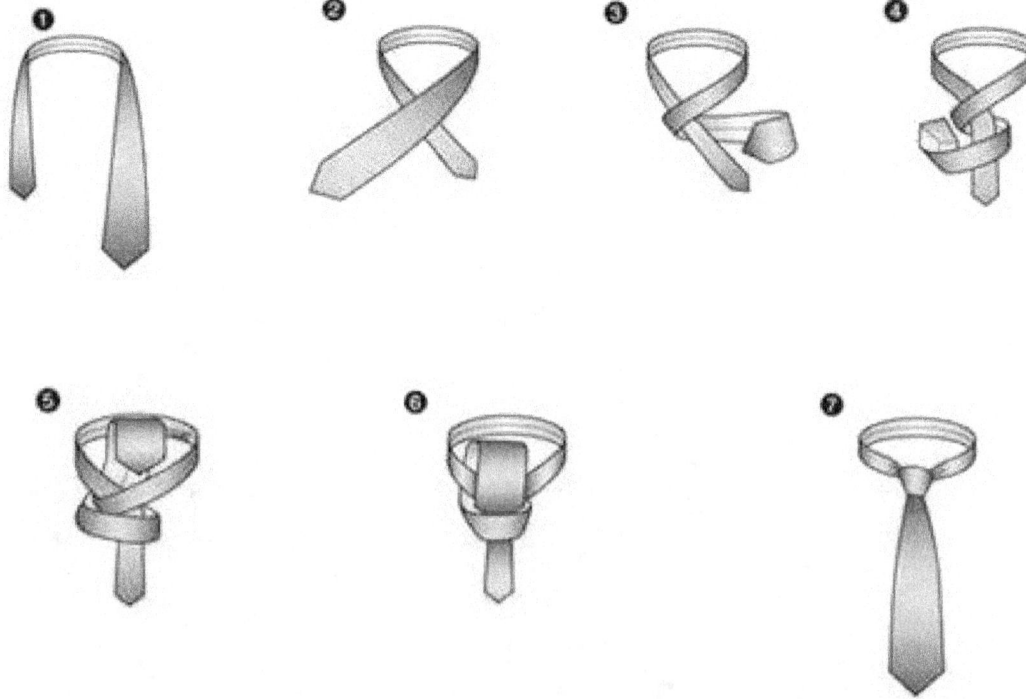

ELDREDGE KNOT

This is a one-of-a-kind knot. To be able to do it, it is necessary to start with the thin part of the tie Unlike the vast majority of tie knots, this knot has a braided shape very similar to a fishtail, it is a quite elegant knot and it will make a great impression everyone who sees it

- Esthetic ☆☆☆☆☆
- Difficulty ☆☆☆☆

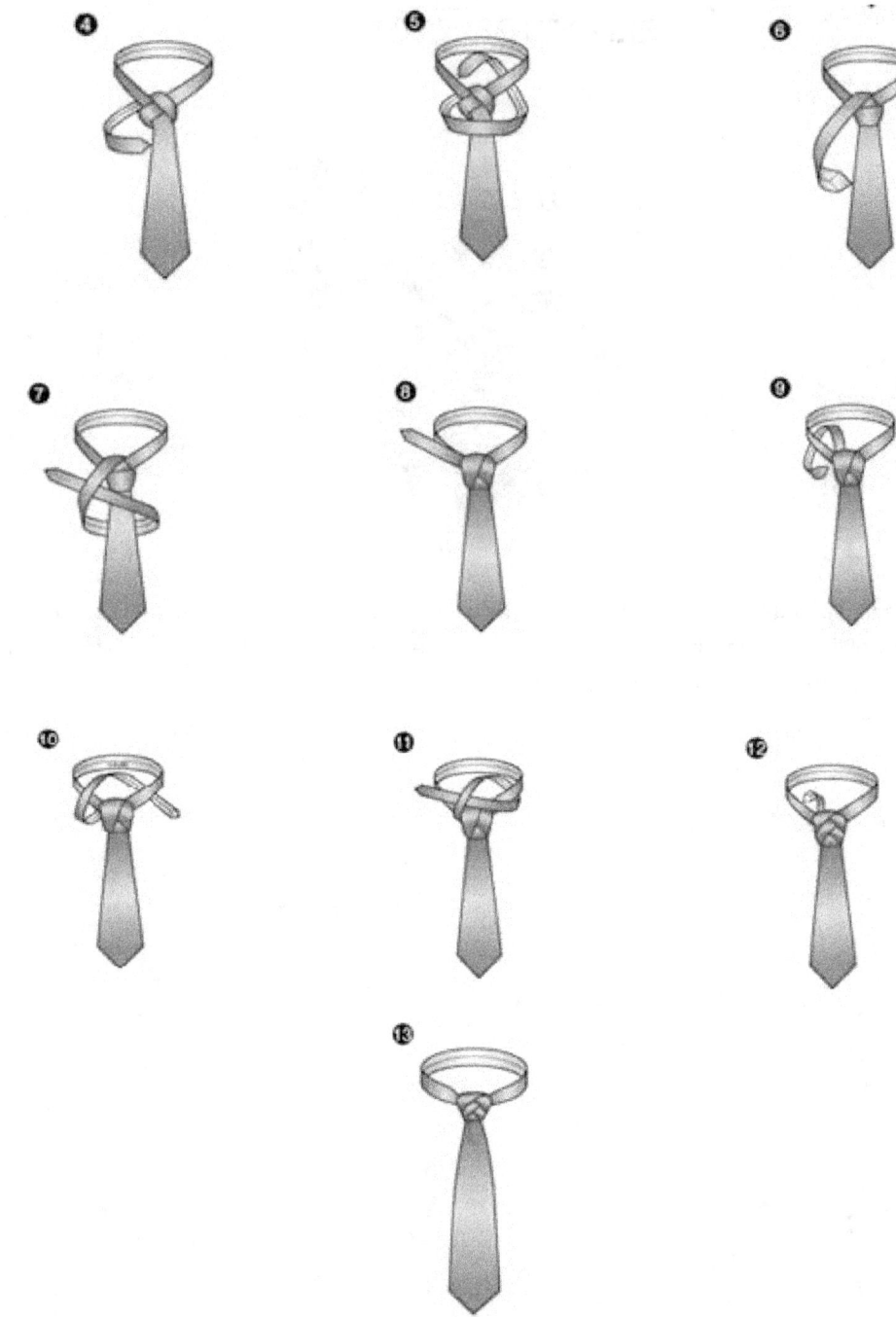

TRINITY KNOT

As its name implies, this knot has three symmetrical routes and brings an air to the Celtic Triquetra. The design converges on a central point, producing a very striking effect. It may seem complicated at first glance, but it is actually quite easy to do.

- Esthetic - ☆☆☆☆
- Difficulty - ☆☆☆☆

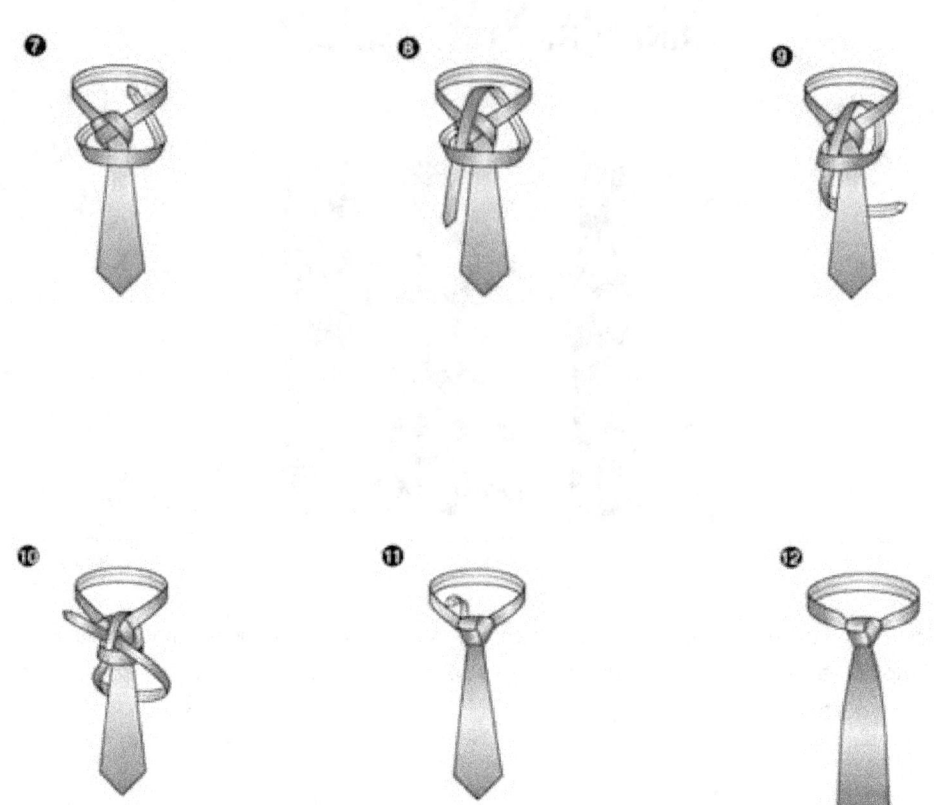

VAN WIJK KNOT

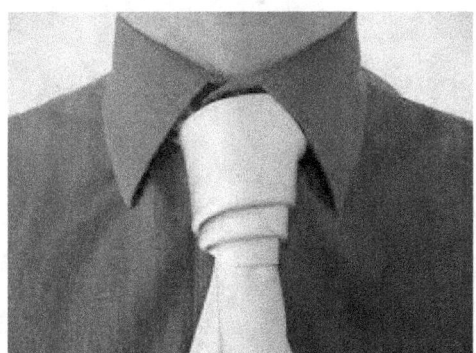

This knot produces a bulky effect in the very own Prince Albert style, by adding a third turn to the narrow end of the tie, this elongated and narrow knot creates a very striking and unmistakable layered cylindrical effect. A very modern knot that is better with light colors. It is best suited for narrow neck shirts and duo with a vest.

- Esthetic - ☆☆☆☆☆
- Difficulty - ☆☆

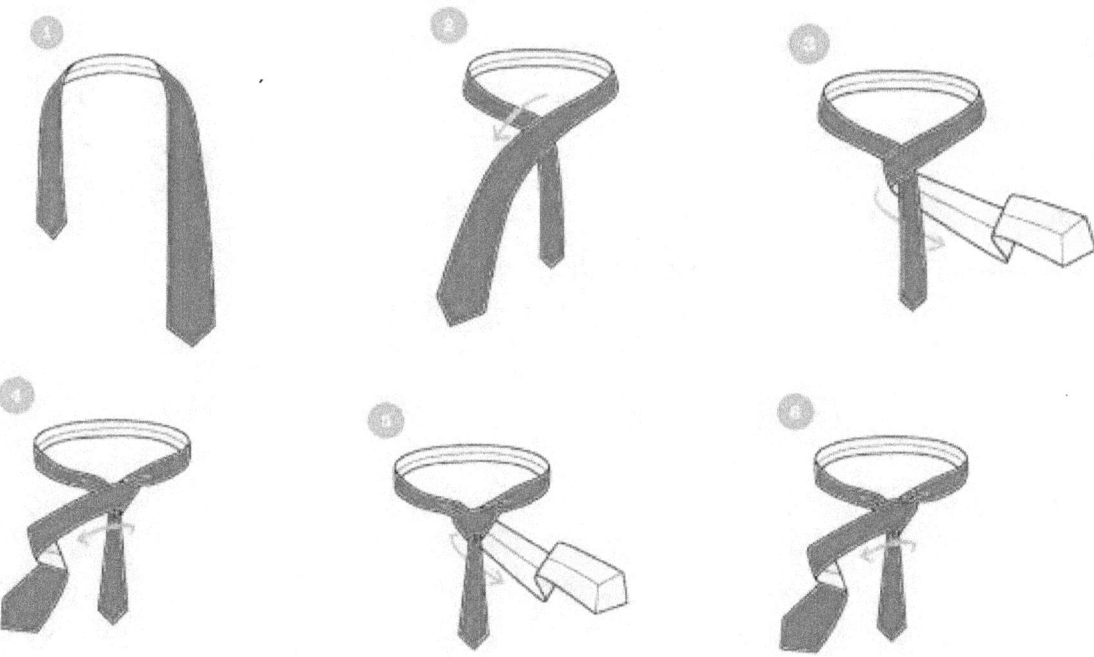

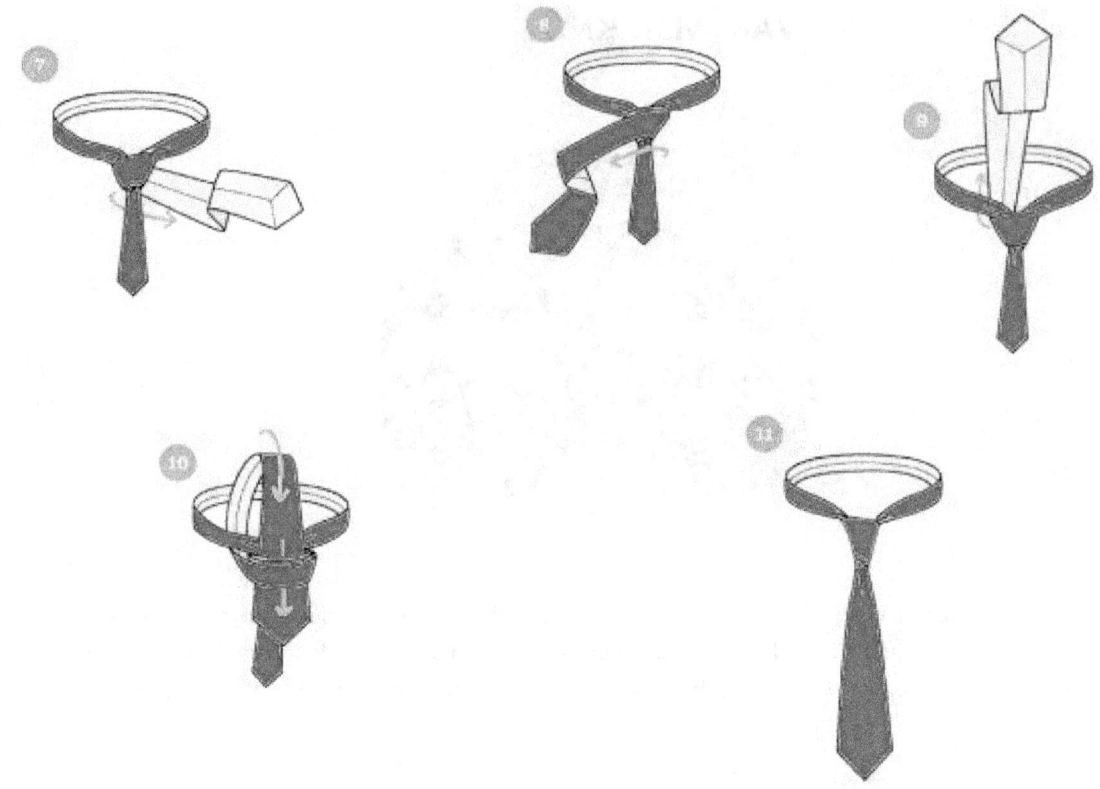

FISH KNOT KNOT

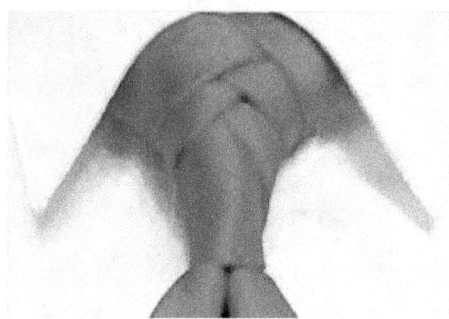

This knot is a bit complicated to make and requires incredible artistic work, as its name implies is shaped like a fish bone. This knot stands out for its elegance, which makes it more and more considerate and makes great impressions for the viewer.

- Esthetic -
- Difficulty -

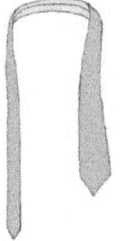 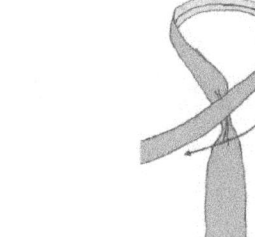 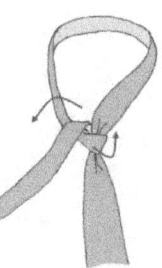

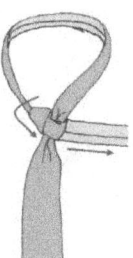 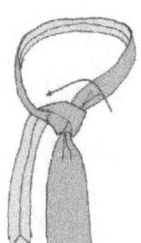 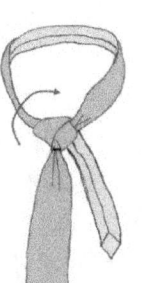

  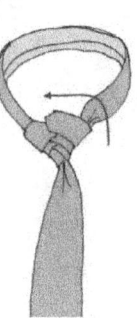

MEROVINGIO KNOT

This knot is original and fans of the movie The Matrix love it for the effect of having two ties, but in reality it is only one, this knot is called the Ediety knot,

- Esthetic - ☆☆☆☆
- Difficulty - ☆☆☆

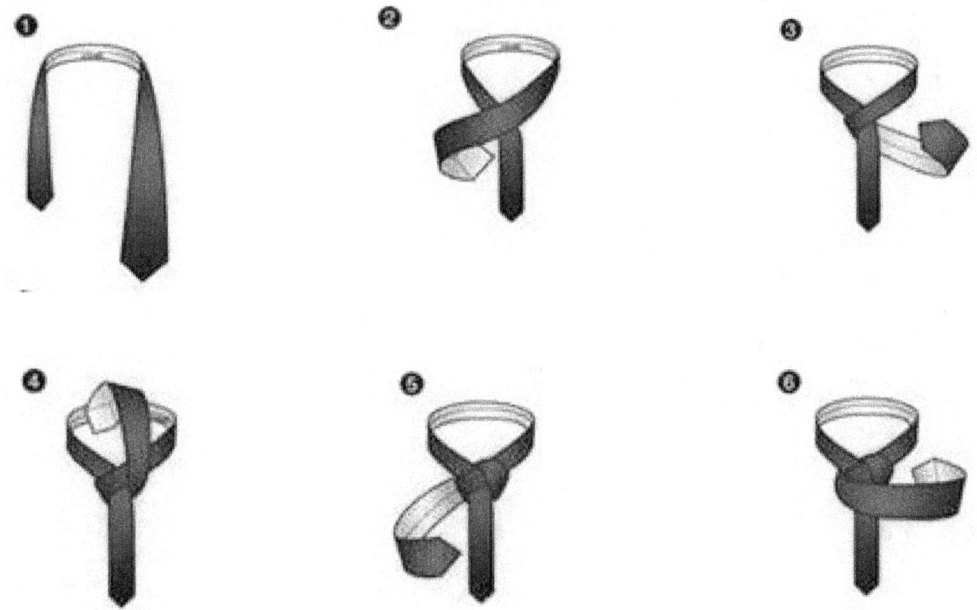

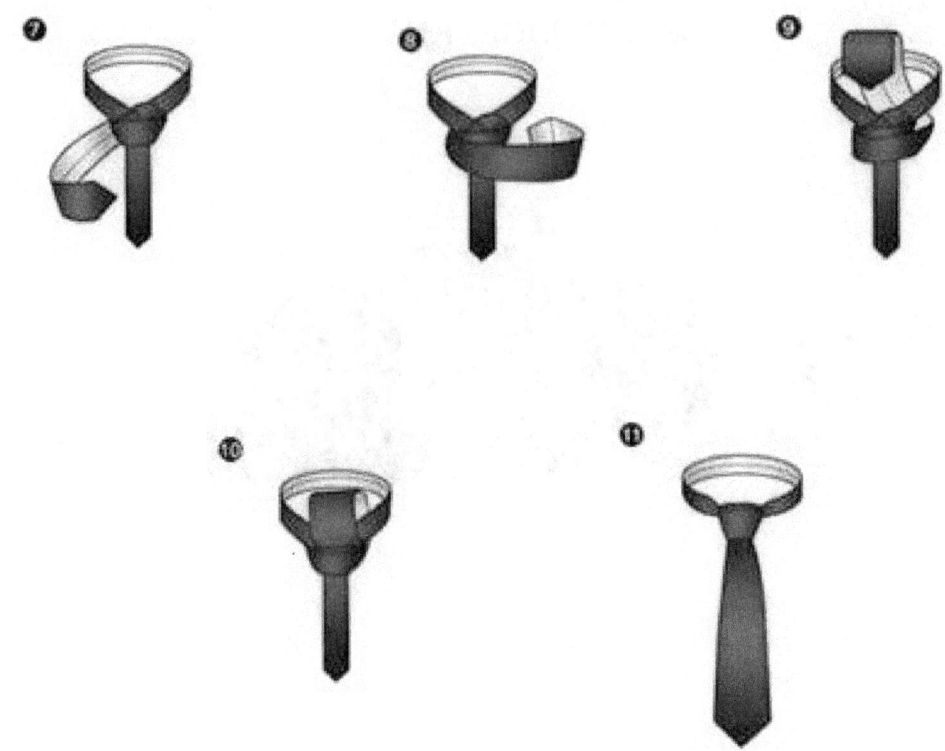

GRANTCHESTER KNOT

The next knot is large, thick, and asymmetrical. This knot is a variant of the St, Andrew knot with a larger size. The secret of this knot is to perform it ideally with a tie made of silk or some type of fabric that is soft to the touch, since being made of other less light materials makes it difficult to make and causes a rough visual effect.

- Esthetic - ★★★☆
- Difficulty - ★★

 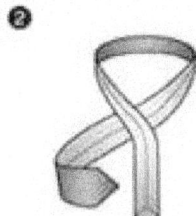 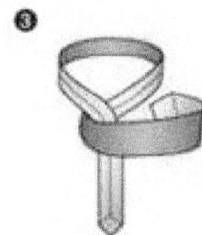

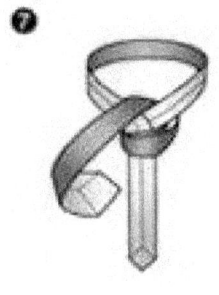
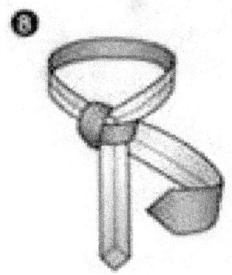
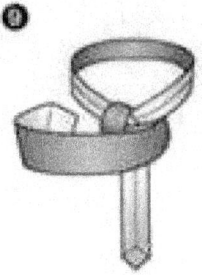
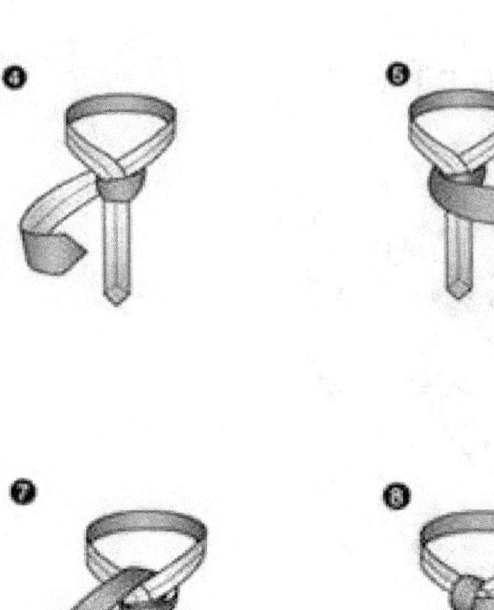
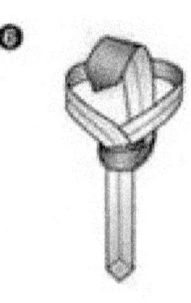
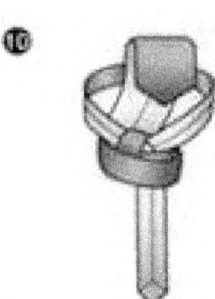

WINDSOR KNOT

It is a knot that generates confidence, elegance and elegance for the business world, it is characterized by being a thick, wide knot with a triangular shape, it is recommended to use for open necks

- Esthetic - ☆☆☆☆☆
- Difficulty - ☆☆☆

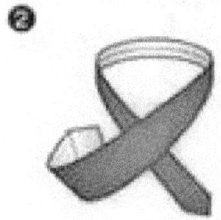
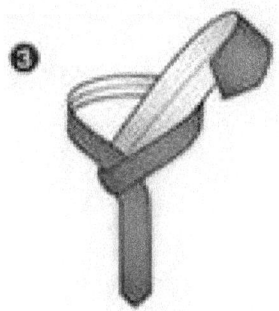

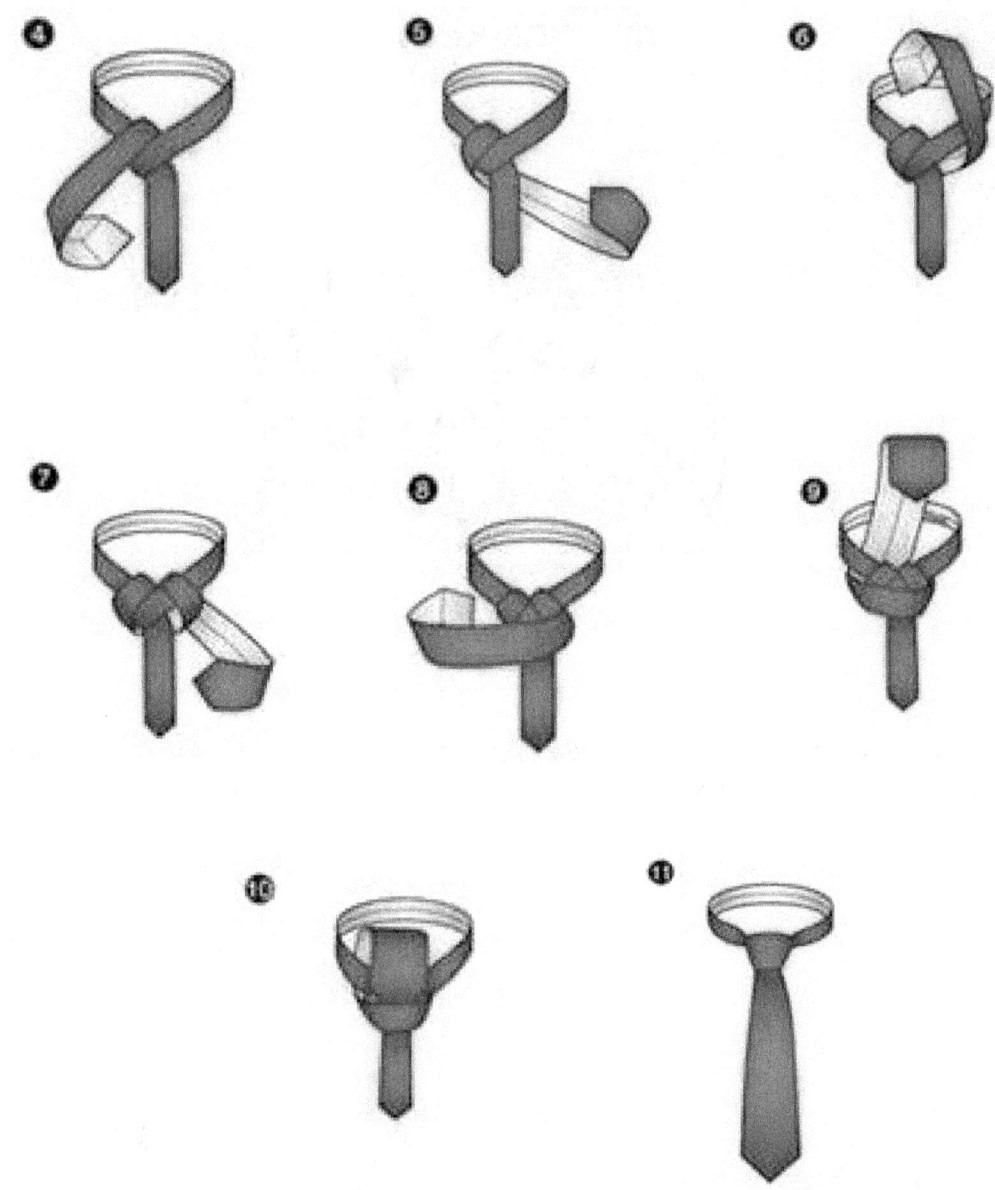

WINDSOR HALF KNOT

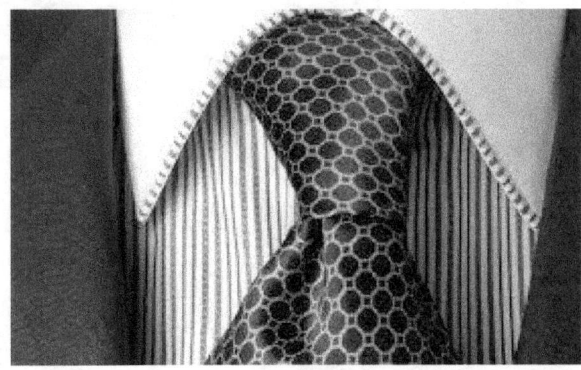

It is a variant of the Windsor knot, it is the most common knot that can be used in different environments such as going to the managerial job or social activities with elegance, if you manage to do it well it will be triangular and symmetrical.

- Esthetic - ☆☆☆
- Difficulty - ☆☆☆

  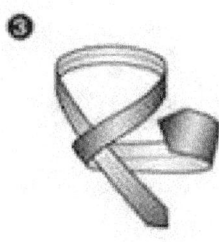

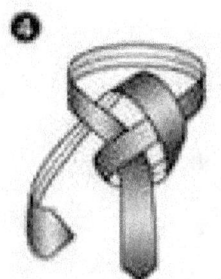

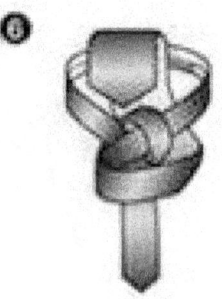
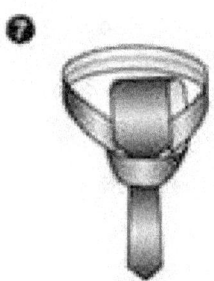

NICKY KNOT

It is an excellent alternative to the pratt knot that requires fewer steps, suitable for medium neck openings, it is characterized by being symmetrical. Ideal for ties made of thicker fabrics for a less bulky look.

- Esthetic - ★★★☆
- Difficulty - ★★

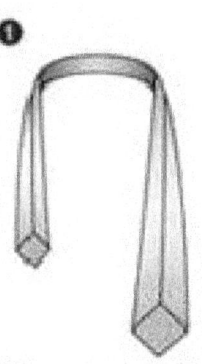
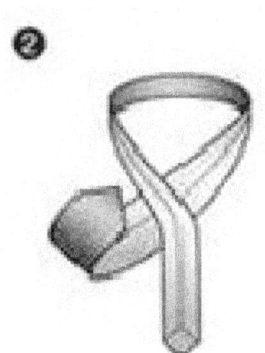

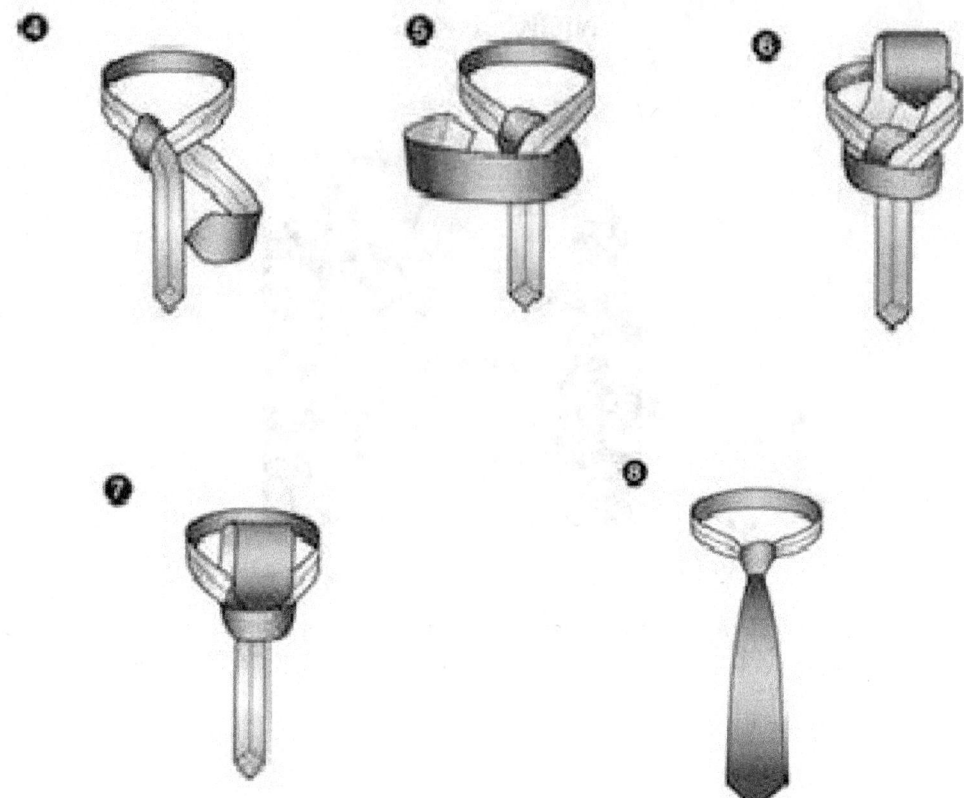

PLATTSBURGH KNOT

Unlike the St. Andrew knot, which is characterized by being symmetrical and highlighted by a wide cone with a narrow and elegant opening, ideal for business dinners or work days. It is recommended to use with knitted or woven ties.

- Esthetic - ☆☆☆☆☆
- Difficulty - ☆☆☆☆

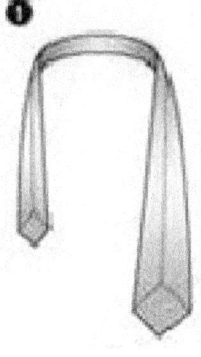 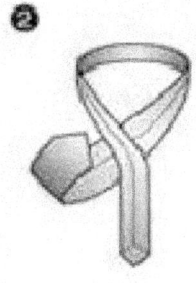 

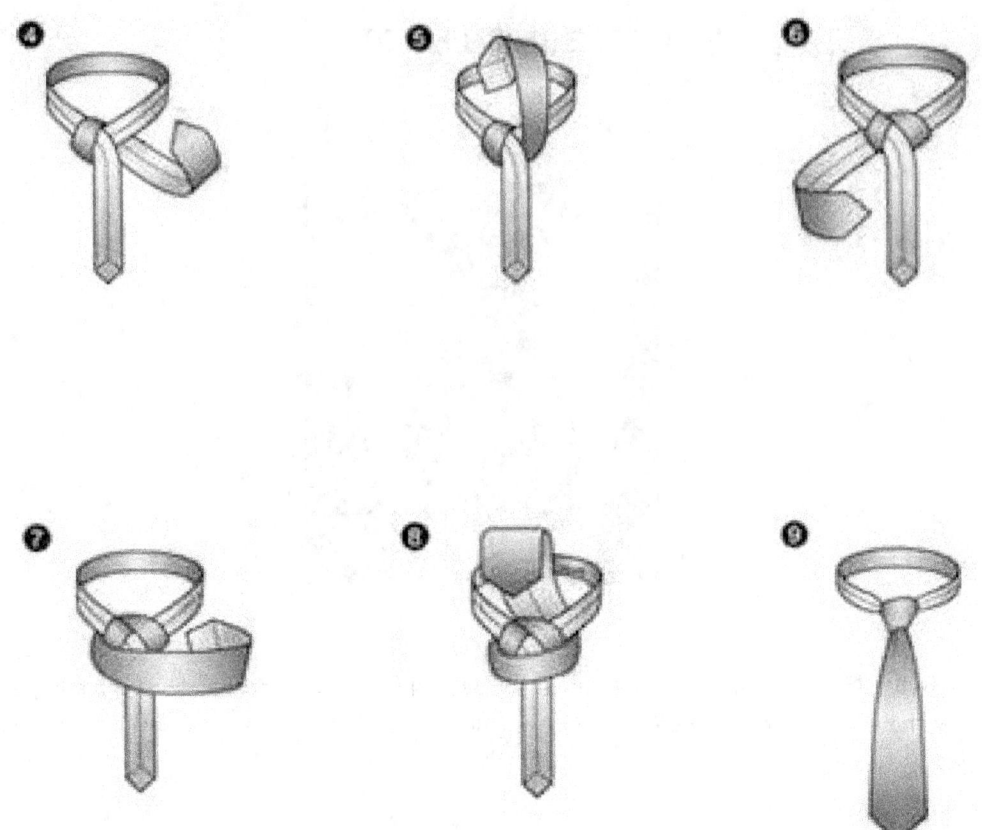

BALTHUS KNOT

This knot is an excellent alternative for ceremonies or formal events such as weddings, it is recommended for cashmere ties, for wide shirt collars and a casual vest. Ideally, the tie should be long because this knot requires more fabric.

- Esthetic - ☆☆☆☆☆
- Difficulty - ☆☆☆

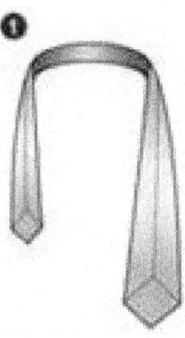 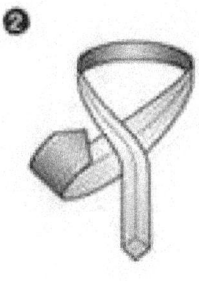 

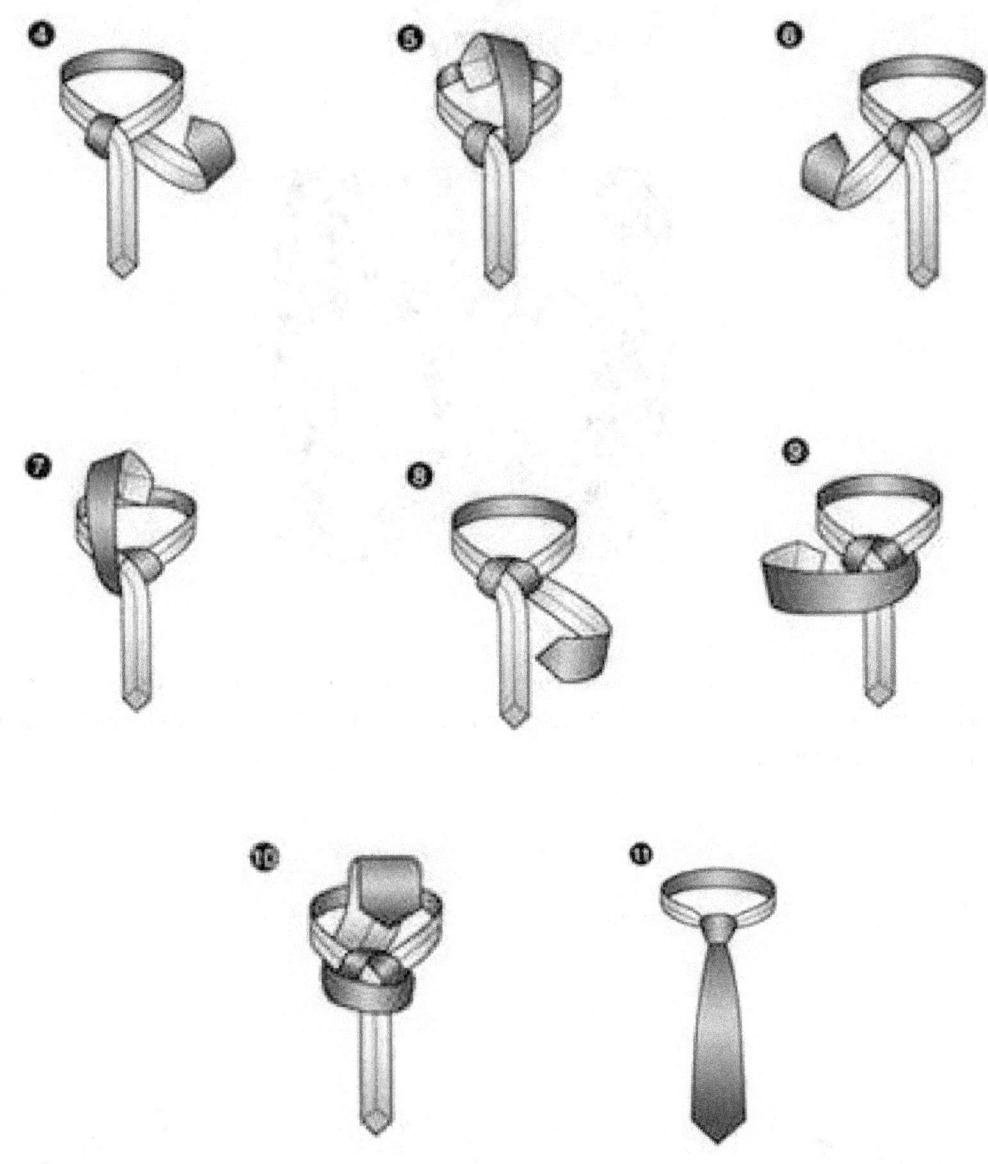

PRATT KNOT

It is a knot that can be used on different occasions, this knot is elegant and medium in size. It can be used with any type of shirts and ideally for wider ties of light and medium fabric. And its main characteristic is discreet.

- Esthetic - ☆☆☆☆
- Difficulty - ☆☆☆

 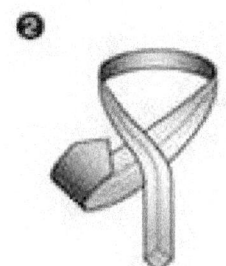 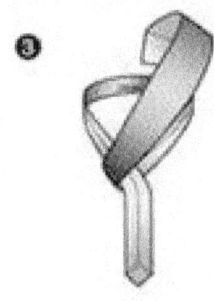

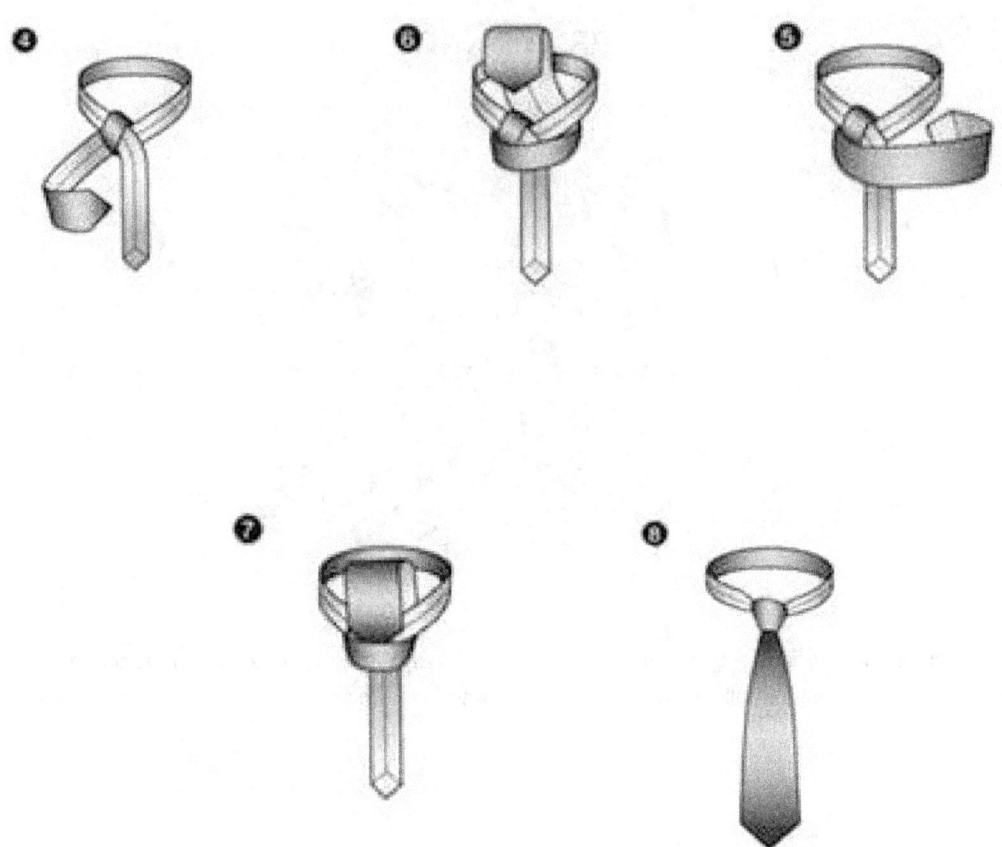

HANNOVER KNOT

With this knot you will be a true gentleman, it is characterized by being large and symmetrical. It is best suited for wide necks, it should be used on long and narrow ties, because it is a large knot. preferably recommended for use with dark ties.

- Esthetic - ☆☆☆☆
- Difficulty - ☆☆☆☆

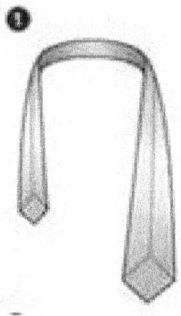 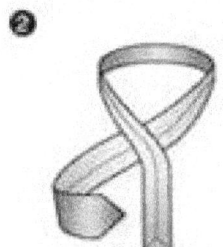 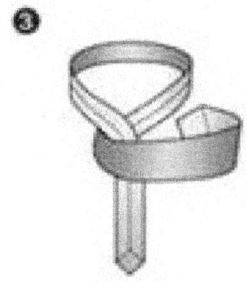

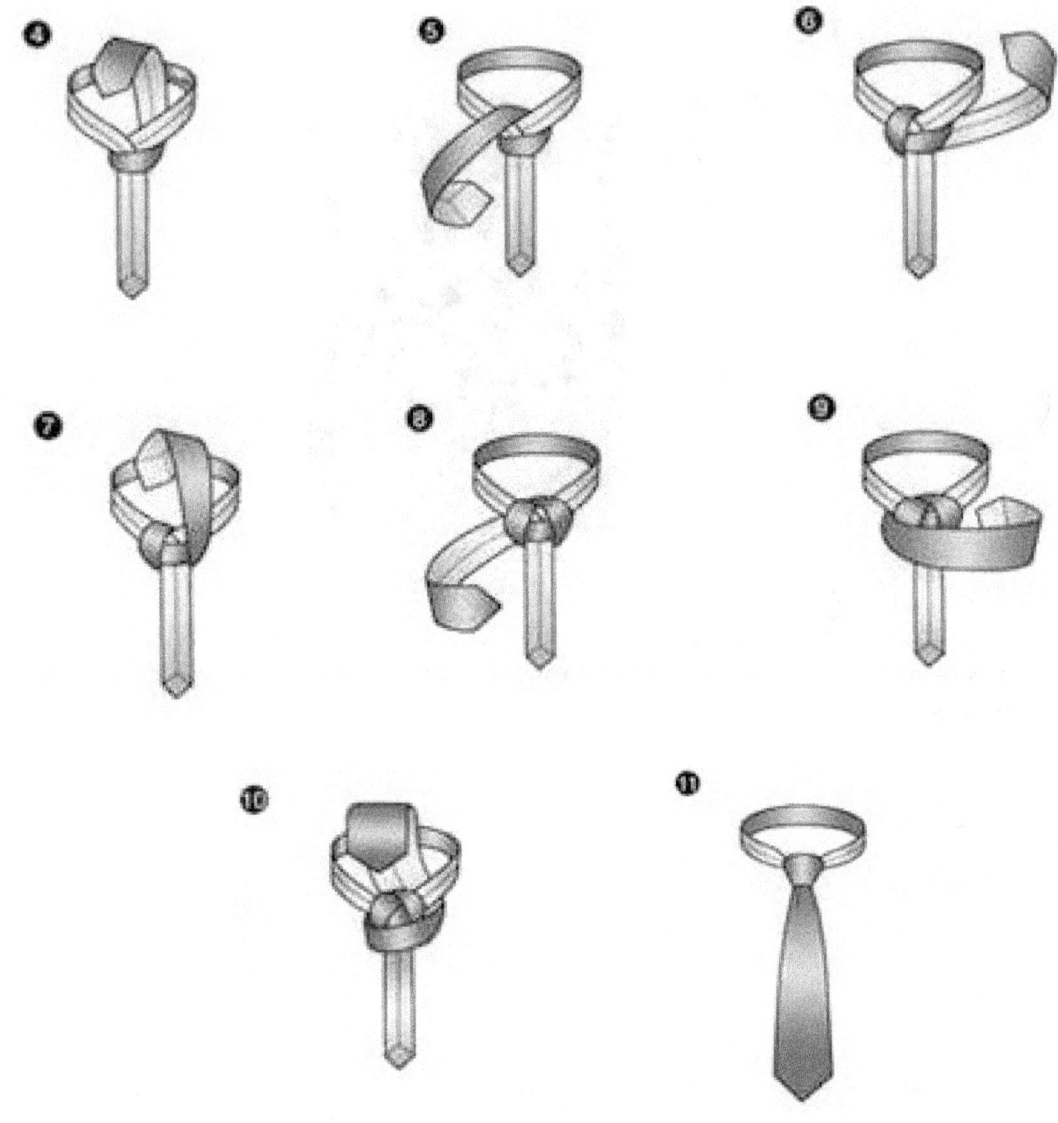

CHRISTENSEN KNOT

It is an elongated, narrow and asymmetrical knot that goes perfectly with narrow neck shirts. It is formal, but with a modern touch. It goes well with any tie design, and is versatile enough to wear for both formal and social events.

- Esthetic - ☆☆☆☆
- Difficulty - ☆☆☆

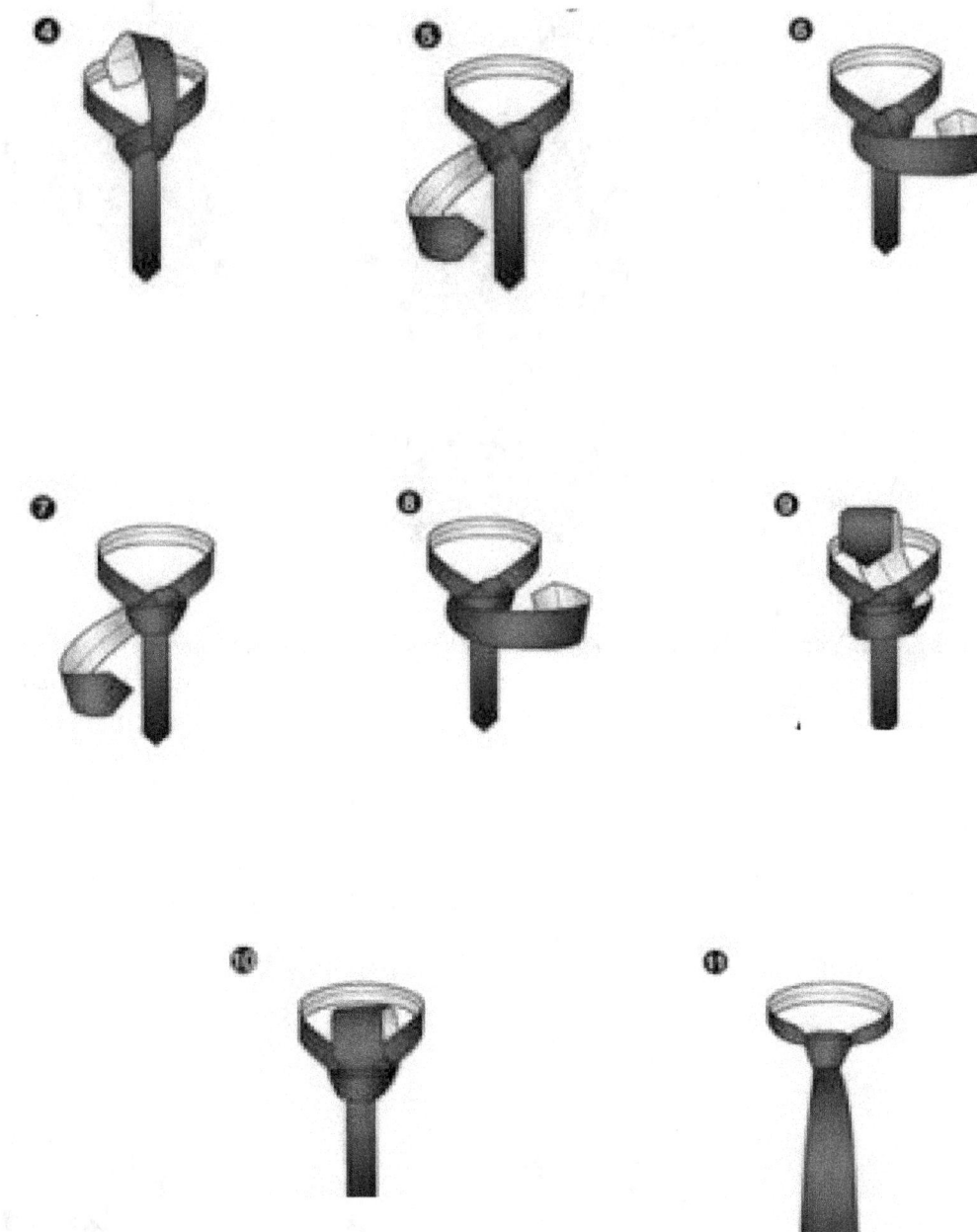

BOW TIE

The bow tie or also called a bow tie, bow tie, bow tie, bow tie, bow tie or humita can be worn by both men and women, becoming a fundamental accessory for elegant clothing, such as the use of Frac and tuxedo. It is a fabric ribbon tied around the neck symmetrically, in such a way that the opposite ends form two loops. Bow ties already tied with a ribbon around the neck and attached with a clip are now available.

- Esthetic - ☆☆☆☆☆
- Difficulty - ☆☆☆

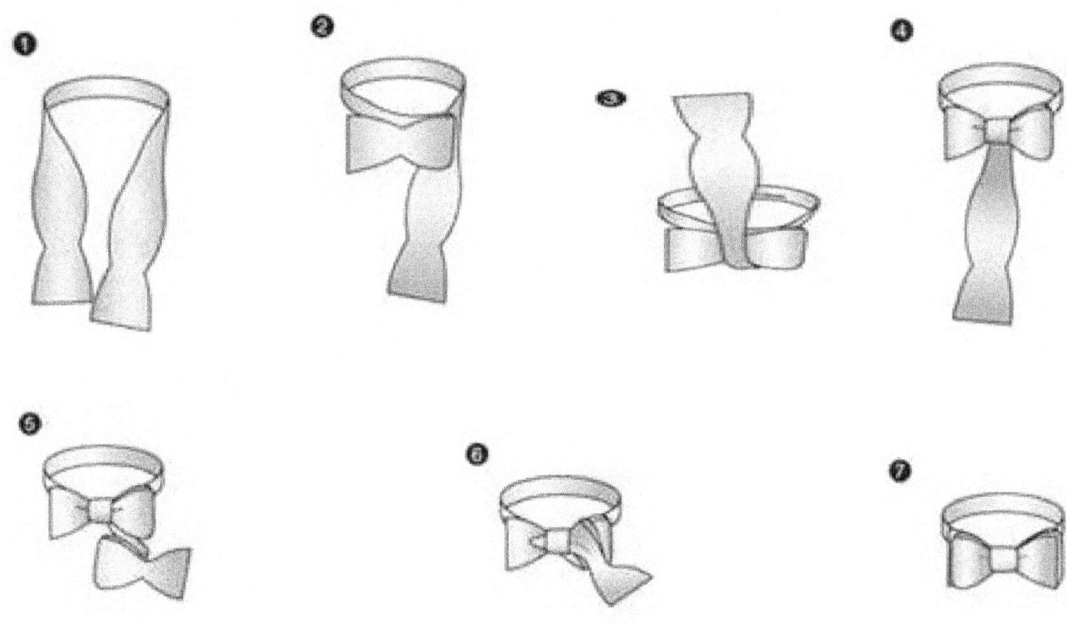

www.ingramcontent.com/pod-product-compliance
Lightning Source LLC
Chambersburg PA
CBHW080439220526

45465CB00009B/3352